FIRST CYBERTRUCK IN THE UK
Issues and Possible Solutions - Everything You Need to Know

A First-Time Owner's Guide to Tesla's Bold Experiment—What Works, What Doesn't, and What They Don't Tell You

J. Andy Peters

Copyright ©**J. Andy Peters, *2024*.**

All rights reserved. No part of this publication may be reproduced, distributed, or transmitted in any form or by any means, including photocopying, recording, or other electronic or mechanical methods, without the prior written permission of the publisher, except in the case of brief quotations embodied in critical reviews and certain other noncommercial uses permitted by copyright law.

Table of Contents

Introduction...4
Chapter 1: The Hype Before the Reality.....................9
Chapter 2: The Initial Excitement...............................16
Chapter 3: Charging Woes.. 23
Chapter 4: Public Perception and Reactions...........30
Chapter 5: What Works and What Doesn't...............37
Chapter 6: The Bold Experiment of Tesla................ 48
Chapter 7: The Ownership Experience.....................57
Dealing with Issues... 62
Financial Aspects.. 65
Chapter 8: Possible Solutions and What Tesla Needs to Improve... 69
Chapter 9: Looking Ahead...78
Conclusion.. 87

Introduction

The Cybertruck has become one of the most talked-about vehicles of the modern age. Its angular, futuristic design, which seems more like something out of a sci-fi movie than a car, has captured the imaginations of millions around the world. When Tesla first revealed it in 2019, it wasn't just a car launch—it was a moment. A bold statement from Elon Musk and Tesla about what the future of transportation could look like. The media frenzy was intense. People either loved it or hated it, but no one could ignore it. There was no middle ground. Some saw it as a brilliant leap into the future, while others dismissed it as an impractical, ugly mess. But regardless of the opinions, one thing was clear: the Cybertruck had everyone talking.

When I first heard that Tesla would be releasing the first Cybertruck to the UK, I couldn't help but feel a rush of excitement. The opportunity to own the first one in the country was a chance to be a part of something historic—something bigger than just owning a car. This wasn't just about getting my hands on a cutting-edge electric vehicle; it was about becoming part of the story, being one of the first people to experience what would soon become a global phenomenon. I wanted to be among the select few who could say they drove the first Cybertruck in the UK, to share in the thrill of taking a step into the unknown. It felt like I was stepping into a new era of automotive design—one that wasn't limited by tradition but instead defined by innovation.

As the days ticked down to the arrival of my Cybertruck, I couldn't help but feel a mix of anticipation and disbelief. There were moments when I thought, "Is this really happening? Am I really about to drive the first one in the UK?" I had followed the launch from the very beginning, watched every update, every teaser video, every reveal. And now, here I was—about to take delivery of a car that felt as revolutionary as the first iPhone.

It was more than just a car; it was a symbol of change.

The reality of owning the first Cybertruck in the UK, however, wasn't as smooth as I imagined. Sure, there was the excitement of being a part of something historic, but with that came a host of challenges, frustrations, and learning curves I wasn't prepared for. I quickly realized that being the first to own something like this wasn't all about the novelty and the attention it brought. There were real-world issues that came with it—problems I hadn't anticipated and didn't expect from a company that had built such a reputation for innovation. The journey of owning the Cybertruck became a personal exploration, not just of the vehicle, but of the process of stepping into a new age of electric cars.

The first time I saw the Cybertruck up close, it was even more striking than I imagined. The raw, angular exterior that had received so much criticism in the media was, in person, even more imposing, more aggressive. But it also felt undeniably futuristic, as if it belonged to a time yet to come. As I sat in the driver's seat for the first time, the excitement was palpable. Yet, that initial thrill was tempered by the realization that there were aspects of the Cybertruck that I hadn't fully understood until I was sitting behind the wheel.

Over time, the excitement shifted. It wasn't just about the newness of owning something no one else had; it was about adapting to the realities of daily life with a vehicle like the Cybertruck. The attention it drew was intense—people on the street stopping to take pictures, to ask questions, to film. But the constant eyes on the truck also meant constant questions. There was the immediate attention from everyone around me, but then there were the more personal struggles of figuring out how to live with the Cybertruck in everyday settings. Charging issues, system bugs, and other technical challenges quickly became a part of my life. They weren't dealbreakers, but they were real problems that I hadn't anticipated.

What started as a thrilling experience became a deeper journey of discovery. The highs were high, but the lows were unexpected. It wasn't just about the car anymore; it was about the experience of owning something so innovative and yet so imperfect. It was a journey of learning, of understanding the potential and limitations of a vehicle that, in many ways, was still ahead of its time. And that journey—like the Cybertruck itself—was far from over.

Chapter 1: The Hype Before the Reality

The first reveal of the Cybertruck was unlike anything the automotive world had ever seen. It was a moment that felt both futuristic and bizarre at the same time. When Elon Musk stepped onto the stage at the Los Angeles Convention Center in November 2019, the world was already brimming with curiosity. Tesla had built a reputation for pushing the boundaries of innovation, but this was something completely new—something that seemed to defy all traditional design principles. Musk had promised the audience a vehicle that would revolutionize the way we think about trucks, and what appeared on that stage was nothing short of radical.

The Cybertruck wasn't just a new electric truck; it was a complete departure from everything that came before it. The body, made of ultra-hard stainless steel, gleamed under the lights with an industrial aesthetic that felt like it belonged on a spaceship rather than the streets of everyday cities.

Its sharp, angular lines and polygonal structure were far from the smooth, rounded curves that had become standard in modern car design. It looked like nothing else on the market—an alien design that seemed too bold, too aggressive to be real. Yet, there it was, sitting on the stage, drawing all eyes to it.

The reactions were immediate and polarizing. On one side, you had the enthusiasts, the die-hard Tesla fans who saw it as the dawn of a new era. They appreciated its unapologetic weirdness, its raw, unfiltered approach to design. To them, the Cybertruck was a symbol of innovation—something that dared to break the rules of the automotive industry. They saw it as a vehicle that wasn't just about utility; it was about pushing boundaries, about shaking up the established norms and doing things differently.

Then there were the critics, who had a very different take. For many car enthusiasts, the Cybertruck's design was a shocking misstep. It was too unconventional, too outlandish. It looked, in the words of some, like a "failed science experiment" or a "boxy, oversized toy." They didn't understand the appeal and found its lack of curves and polished design a hard pill to swallow. The Cybertruck didn't just go against the grain—it seemed to mock the very idea of what a truck should look like. It was, for many, simply too strange to take seriously.

Yet, amidst the criticism and praise, one thing remained clear: the Cybertruck had people talking. It was impossible to ignore. The electric vehicle market, which had traditionally been associated with sleek, refined designs, now had a contender that was rough, rugged, and downright rebellious. Whether you loved it or hated it, the Cybertruck had made an impression. And in the world of automotive design, that's all that matters.

For me, watching the reveal was like seeing the future unfold before my eyes. I saw a truck that wasn't afraid to stand out, a truck that embodied the kind of boldness and vision that made Tesla so revolutionary. It wasn't perfect, but it was definitely something that would make waves. And I couldn't wait to be a part of it.

The Cybertruck is more than just another vehicle; it's a bold experiment in the world of automobiles, a daring leap into uncharted territory for Tesla and the entire automotive industry. In many ways, it's a test case for the future of car design, functionality, and technology—one that challenges preconceived notions of what a truck should be and what a vehicle can do. From its rugged, geometric exoskeleton to its electric powertrain, the Cybertruck represents a complete departure from everything we've come to expect from traditional cars. Tesla, known for its ability to innovate, took a gamble with the Cybertruck, and in doing so, pushed the boundaries of what's possible in vehicle design.

The design itself is perhaps the most striking feature of the Cybertruck. Unlike anything else on the road, the truck's angular, almost fortress-like exterior challenges every design norm that has governed vehicles for decades. It's a truck built for strength, durability, and practicality—an aesthetic choice that's as functional as it is unconventional. The body is made from an ultra-hard stainless steel, a material that Musk himself has called "bulletproof." Tesla claims this metal is not only nearly indestructible but also gives the vehicle a distinctive look that sets it apart from everything else on the market. In a world where every truck seems to blend into the same mold, the Cybertruck stands as an outlier, boldly proclaiming that being different isn't just okay—it's the future.

Then there's the technological side of things. Tesla made a number of ambitious promises about the Cybertruck's capabilities, and many of them are truly groundbreaking. It's designed to be not only an electric truck but a workhorse capable of performing the tough tasks that traditionally defined pickups: hauling, towing, and navigating challenging terrain. With its impressive range, off-road capability, and towing capacity, the Cybertruck is poised to compete with some of the toughest gas-powered trucks on the market, but with a completely green footprint. Tesla also promised a fully autonomous driving system, further pushing the envelope on what a truck can do in terms of technological sophistication.

But what really drew me in was the sheer audacity of the Cybertruck. It wasn't just a vehicle; it was a vision of what the future could look like. As someone who has always been fascinated by technology, innovation, and the way the world is changing, the Cybertruck felt like a symbol of progress—a vehicle that wasn't afraid to be different, a vehicle that was about more than just getting from point A to point B. It was about making a statement, about embracing a bold new future where the limits were pushed further than ever before.

From the moment I saw that first reveal, I was captivated. I wasn't just intrigued by the truck's potential; I was drawn to its promise of a better, cleaner, and more efficient way to live with our vehicles. Tesla's promises of innovation—of groundbreaking technology, a sustainable future, and a design that boldly said "this is not like anything you've ever seen"—were all too compelling to ignore. I knew this was the kind of vehicle that would forever change the way we think about driving, technology, and the very idea of what a car could be. It was a vision of the future, and I wanted to be part of it.

Chapter 2: The Initial Excitement

When the day finally arrived, I couldn't believe it. After months of waiting, watching updates, and tracking every news article about the Cybertruck, I was about to receive the first model in the UK. The anticipation had reached its peak. I had secured my place in history, or so it felt, as the first person to own a Cybertruck in the country. The excitement was palpable, not just for me, but for everyone around me who knew how much this moment meant. It wasn't just about getting a new car—it was about being part of something revolutionary. This was the future of transportation, and I was about to step into it.

The delivery process was like no other I had experienced. There were no traditional car dealership interactions, no showroom banter, or haggling over prices. It was just me and Tesla, a company I had admired for years, finally making this moment happen. As the delivery truck rolled up, I couldn't help but feel like a kid on Christmas morning. When the Cybertruck was unloaded, it stood there—unmistakably bold, impossibly angular, and completely unlike anything I had ever seen before. My heart raced as I approached it, almost in disbelief that this was now my vehicle. The setup was simple but exciting; I was handed the keys, the paperwork, and the software login for the car's integrated systems, and just like that, I was ready to hit the road.

Getting behind the wheel of the Cybertruck was surreal. The interior felt just as futuristic as the exterior, with its minimalist design and cutting-edge technology. The dashboard was dominated by a massive touchscreen display, offering access to virtually every function of the vehicle. It was a far cry from the more traditional layouts of most cars, but there was something elegant and intuitive about it. The seats were comfortable, with a clean, industrial design that complemented the truck's exterior. I felt like I had stepped into a machine built for the future, not just a car, but an experience.

Driving the Cybertruck for the first time was like stepping into another dimension. The moment I pressed the accelerator, I was amazed at how smooth and powerful it felt, despite the truck's bulky appearance. There was no engine roar, no vibrations typical of conventional trucks. Instead, it moved with an electric hum, gliding effortlessly through the streets. Its size was initially intimidating—after all, it's a massive vehicle. But the handling was surprisingly agile, and the sharp, boxy design somehow made it feel more connected to the road than I had anticipated. Every turn, every shift in speed, felt deliberate and direct. The futuristic design of the truck wasn't just for show—it translated into real, functional driving experience that set it apart from anything else on the road.

But it wasn't just the driving experience that impressed me. The Cybertruck felt like a complete reinvention of what a vehicle could be. It wasn't just about transporting you from point A to point B; it was about the experience, the innovation, and the sheer thrill of driving something that felt ahead of its time. And in that moment, I couldn't help but feel a sense of pride. I wasn't just driving a car; I was driving a statement. A glimpse into what the future of mobility could look like. It felt special, not just because it was the first Cybertruck in the UK, but because it was a vehicle that promised to change everything we thought we knew about trucks and electric vehicles.

Every time I got behind the wheel, it felt like I was driving the future. The Cybertruck wasn't just a vehicle; it was a glimpse into the next chapter of automotive history, and I was lucky enough to be a part of it.

As soon as I hit the streets with the Cybertruck, it became clear that this vehicle was unlike anything people had ever seen before. The reactions were instant and, at times, overwhelming. It wasn't just the size of the truck that turned heads—it was the way it seemed to defy every traditional design convention. Everywhere I drove, eyes followed me. People slowed down in their cars to get a better look, pedestrians stopped in their tracks, and some even pulled out their phones to snap pictures or record videos. It was as though the Cybertruck wasn't just a vehicle on the road—it was an event, a spectacle.

I remember one afternoon, driving through a busy town center, when a group of people gathered around, asking questions almost as if I had just stepped out of a spaceship. They were fascinated, eager to learn everything about it, from how it drove to what it was made of. It wasn't just curiosity—it was amazement. Some people were genuinely excited about the possibilities of the vehicle, while others, more skeptical, couldn't quite wrap their heads around it. "Is this real?" one person asked as they filmed the truck. "It looks like something from a video game!" another said, clearly in awe of its sharp, unconventional lines.

I couldn't help but smile. There was something about being behind the wheel of a vehicle that elicited such strong reactions—something that made every drive feel like a moment in history. The more I drove it, the more I realized just how much attention it attracted. It wasn't just that the vehicle was electric, or that it was a Tesla; it was the fact that the Cybertruck made people stop and question everything they thought they knew about cars. It was as if the vehicle itself was saying, "This is the future, and you're witnessing it right now."

But not all the reactions were positive. Some people, especially those more accustomed to traditional trucks or sedans, were puzzled. "That thing looks like an upside-down skip," one person quipped as I drove past. It was a reminder that the Cybertruck's design wasn't just unconventional—it was polarizing. Some loved it for its boldness; others couldn't stand it for the same reason. But what was clear was that no one could ignore it. Everyone had an opinion. And that, in itself, felt like a victory for Tesla and for anyone willing to take a step into the unknown.

Chapter 3: Charging Woes

The first time I attempted to charge the Cybertruck, I expected it to be a straightforward process—after all, I had charged plenty of electric vehicles before. Tesla's reputation for simplicity and ease of use was one of the reasons I was so drawn to the brand in the first place. But as I pulled into the charging station, ready to plug in the Cybertruck and watch the percentage climb, things quickly became... less than smooth.

For one, the Cybertruck's sheer size made the process a little more complicated than I had anticipated. I found myself awkwardly maneuvering around the charging station, trying to position the truck just right so the cable could reach. The charging port, hidden behind a sleek, flush panel, wasn't immediately obvious—another small detail that took me a moment to figure out. It wasn't until I saw another driver struggle with the same issue that I realized this was part of the experience—navigating the quirks of a vehicle that's as different as the Cybertruck.

Once I finally had the cable plugged in, I expected everything to work as it should. But then the error message flashed up on the screen: *Charging Error—No Power*. My heart sank for a moment. I'd seen Tesla owners encounter minor charging issues before, but I never imagined it would happen to me, especially with the first Cybertruck in the UK. I double-checked everything: the connection, the charging station itself, and the truck's software. Still, nothing. A few more attempts to restart the process, and the same error message appeared. My battery percentage, which had already dipped to 12%, was barely moving. Panic started to set in. I had purchased this cutting-edge vehicle, but here I was—unable to even get it to charge.

In the midst of this frustration, a small crowd started to gather, no doubt curious about the strange sight of the Cybertruck at the charging station. Some of them asked if I was having trouble.

"Is that the first one?" one person asked, peering at the truck with a mix of awe and confusion. "It's supposed to be all high-tech, right? What's going on?" They were friendly, but I could tell they were watching intently, as though they, too, were waiting to see what would happen next. It wasn't just my moment—it felt like a public spectacle.

I eventually had to call Tesla support. They guided me through the steps of troubleshooting, and after what felt like an eternity of back-and-forth, I finally managed to get the charge working—though it was only a small trickle. The frustration of that first charging attempt was a reminder that, no matter how advanced a vehicle is, there's always a learning curve. It was humbling. And yet, despite the setback, I couldn't help but feel a strange sense of pride. I was navigating this new world of electric vehicles, pushing through the glitches, and figuring it out as I went along. It wasn't a perfect start, but it was all part of the experience. After all, with something this groundbreaking, the journey was just as important as the destination.

The charging issues persisted longer than I had hoped, and the more I tried to troubleshoot, the more my frustration grew. The charging port would click into place, but each time I attempted to initiate the charge, I was greeted with the same cryptic error message: *Charging Error*. At first, I chalked it up to a simple glitch, something minor that could be fixed with a reset or a quick call to customer support. But as the minutes stretched into hours and my battery percentage continued to plummet, I realized this was no ordinary hiccup.

I decided to try everything I could think of. I unhooked the charging cable and plugged it back in, hoping it was just a loose connection. When that didn't work, I attempted to restart the truck's system through the touchscreen. No luck. It was becoming clear that this wasn't going to be a quick fix. I even checked the charging station itself—was it malfunctioning? But when I tried a different stall,

I encountered the same issue. The truck simply wouldn't charge.

As the hours wore on, I started to feel like I was in over my head. It was one of those moments when you realize that no amount of research, no number of online tutorials, or forums was going to solve the problem in real time. At this point, I was considering everything—from calling Tesla's roadside assistance to just towing the thing to the nearest Tesla Service Center. I could feel the weight of being a "first owner" in the UK, the pressure of dealing with an issue that I knew others would soon encounter. Still, I pushed forward, determined to figure it out.

The breakthrough came when I realized that the issue might not be the truck itself, but rather the way I was approaching the charging stations. The Cybertruck, being so new and distinct in its design, had a few idiosyncrasies that didn't align with the typical EV charging infrastructure. I started to focus more on the software side—maybe a software update had just rolled out that hadn't reached my truck yet. I connected it to the Wi-Fi and, sure enough, a prompt appeared on the screen asking if I wanted to install a new update. After a few minutes, I did the same charging routine, and to my surprise, this time it worked.

It was a relief to finally see the battery percentage increase. But the experience had left me with some important lessons. First, while the Cybertruck may be cutting-edge, it's not immune to the teething problems that come with any new technology. Second, I learned that as an early adopter, there's a certain level of patience required. Sometimes things will not work as seamlessly as we hope, especially when dealing with new systems and hardware. And lastly, it became clear that patience with Tesla's software updates is crucial—things often need a few tweaks here and there before everything starts running smoothly.

For anyone else picking up a Cybertruck—or any new Tesla model, for that matter—be prepared to face some bumps along the way. Don't be discouraged if you run into problems, particularly with charging. It's a learning curve, but with the right mindset and a bit of persistence, you'll figure it out. Be sure to keep your truck connected to Wi-Fi to receive the latest updates and be ready to troubleshoot when necessary. Tesla's customer support is responsive, but sometimes, the solution is just a matter of being patient and giving the system time to adjust. If all else fails, don't hesitate to reach out for help—it's all part of the experience.

Chapter 4: Public Perception and Reactions

As I drove the Cybertruck through the streets of the UK, it felt like I was rolling a piece of modern art through a city of skeptics. The reactions were as varied as the vehicle itself—some loved it, some hated it, and others were simply too curious to ignore. Everywhere I went, people stared, took photos, and whispered to each other. I'd never experienced anything like it with any other car I'd owned, and it became clear that the Cybertruck wasn't just a vehicle; it was a conversation starter.

There were definitely those who were in awe, marveling at its boldness. I'd often pull up to a stoplight, only to see the driver in the car next to me staring with wide eyes. Some would roll down their windows, lean out, and shout, "That's insane!" or "Is that real?!" It was almost as if they couldn't believe something so unconventional was actually on the road. There were even a few people who, in their excitement, would follow me for a while, snapping pictures as if they were documenting a rare species in the wild. I could feel the pride in being the one driving it—this wasn't just a truck, it was an experience, and everyone around me seemed to recognize that.

On the other hand, there were the critics—the ones who just didn't get it. I remember one instance where I parked in a busy shopping area, and as I stepped out of the truck, I overheard a group of people discussing it. "It looks like a tin can," one said. "Who would ever drive something that looks like that?" another added, shaking their head in disbelief. For them, the Cybertruck was a monstrosity, a design nightmare that had no place on the streets. They couldn't understand why anyone would choose a vehicle that seemed so out of place with the traditional, sleek lines of most modern cars. It was clear they were uncomfortable with how different it was, and to be honest, I could understand their point of view. The Cybertruck was loud in its silence, and for some, that was just too much.

But then there were those in the middle—curious, questioning, intrigued. They didn't love it, but they didn't hate it either. They were fascinated by its audacity. They'd ask questions, snap a quick picture, and then move on, perhaps wondering if one day they, too, would drive something so radical. "How does it drive?" one man asked as he walked past, peering inside. "Is it like a regular truck?" Another person wanted to know how it performed in the rain, which made me laugh a little—this was a vehicle so unlike anything they'd seen that even the most basic questions seemed to carry weight.

The truth is, the Cybertruck sparked reactions wherever it went—strong, conflicting, and full of curiosity. Whether love or hate, everyone had something to say about it. And for me, that was part of the thrill: the Cybertruck wasn't just a car, it was a catalyst for conversation. It forced people to reconsider what a vehicle could be, and that, in itself, was a kind of success.

As the first Cybertruck in the UK made its way through the streets, there was an interesting—and somewhat amusing—misconception that seemed to follow it wherever it went. Because of all the hype surrounding Tesla and the Cybertruck's dramatic reveal, many people assumed that the vehicle I was driving wasn't really a "real" model at all. They thought it was some sort of promotional stunt, a special edition sent out for marketing purposes rather than an actual, functioning vehicle. "Is this just for show?" one passerby asked me at a traffic light, his tone skeptical, as if he couldn't believe anyone would actually own such an outlandish truck.

This confusion wasn't entirely unfounded. After all, in the early days, Tesla had made headlines by sending prototype vehicles to certain high-profile figures for promotional purposes. So when the Cybertruck arrived on UK soil, many people couldn't shake the idea that it was just another flashy marketing tool, perhaps meant to drum up more attention before the actual release. Some even speculated that it wasn't roadworthy—that it might still be a prototype in the testing phase. It didn't help that I was driving it around in the very early stages of its availability, when only a handful of people outside of Tesla's inner circle had even seen it in person.

But no, this wasn't a marketing stunt—it was *my* Cybertruck, and yes, it was very much real. There was a sense of pride in clearing up that misconception, but at the same time, it made me realize just how much the vehicle had become a symbol, almost more than just a mode of transportation. For some, it wasn't just a truck; it was something to be seen, something to be admired or questioned.

In a way, it was almost like the Cybertruck itself had become a celebrity. Everywhere it went, it generated buzz, and I was merely its driver, an unintentional bystander in the spectacle it created. When I pulled up to a café or parked in front of a store, I noticed people gathering around, phones raised high, eager to get a shot of the truck. It wasn't like any other car where people might glance over and move on. No, this was an event. Kids would point excitedly, asking their parents what kind of car it was, while adults would whisper to each other, trying to make sense of what they were seeing. There was an undeniable aura of celebrity surrounding the Cybertruck—like it was something out of a futuristic movie, something almost too outlandish to be real. Some people approached me just to ask about it, others to take selfies, and a few even joked about how they were witnessing "the future of cars."

I became somewhat of an unofficial tour guide for the truck, explaining its features and quirks to anyone who was curious enough to stop and ask. And I quickly realized that this wasn't just a vehicle—it was a conversation piece, a status symbol, and for many, an aspirational glimpse into the future of transportation. It wasn't about the practicality or even the design anymore—it was about the experience of *witnessing* something new, something revolutionary.

Chapter 5: What Works and What Doesn't

Driving the Cybertruck for the first time was an experience that left me in awe of its raw power and unique handling. The performance of this vehicle is unlike any truck I've driven before, electric or otherwise. With its all-electric powertrain, the Cybertruck is deceptively fast for something so large and imposing. Despite its rugged appearance, it has the acceleration of a high-performance sports car. Tesla claims that the top-tier version can accelerate from 0 to 60 mph in just 2.9 seconds, and I can confirm that the rush of speed is as thrilling as it sounds. Every press of the pedal feels like a jolt of energy, and the torque is instantaneous—there's no lag, no waiting for the engine to wind up. It's immediate, and that's something that continues to surprise me each time I drive.

But it's not just about speed. The Cybertruck's handling is equally impressive, especially given its size. For a truck that weighs well over 2,000 kg and has a distinctly larger footprint than most vehicles on the road, it corners with a surprising level of precision. The low center of gravity, courtesy of the battery pack mounted along the bottom, helps stabilize the vehicle, making it feel planted and controlled, even at higher speeds or when taking tight corners. There's no sense of heaviness or clumsiness—this thing handles like a much smaller vehicle, which is a testament to the genius of Tesla's engineering.

Despite its large stature, the Cybertruck is also surprisingly nimble. It has an adaptive air suspension system that helps smooth out bumps in the road, which makes for a surprisingly comfortable ride, even on rougher terrain. Whether navigating city streets or cruising down the motorway, the Cybertruck performs with confidence and ease. Its electric nature also means that the ride is incredibly quiet, with little to no engine noise, creating a serene driving experience. I expected the Cybertruck to feel cumbersome on the road, but instead, it felt like a powerful and refined machine—one that could easily hold its own against traditional petrol-powered trucks, while offering the added benefits of electric efficiency.

When it comes to practicality, however, the Cybertruck is a bit of a mixed bag. On one hand, it's a truck built to haul, tow, and get things done. The bed is massive, offering more than enough space for large items. Tesla has designed the bed to be both durable and highly functional, with features like a lockable tonneau cover and integrated storage options. Whether I'm hauling tools, sports equipment, or just bags of groceries, I know the Cybertruck can handle it. The truck bed is wide and long, able to carry anything you throw at it, making it perfect for larger loads.

But practicality isn't just about size—it's also about how the vehicle fits into your day-to-day life. And here's where things get a little tricky. While the Cybertruck's exterior is undeniably cool, it's not the easiest vehicle to park or maneuver in tight spaces, especially if you live in an urban area. The sheer size of the truck means that it requires more room than a typical sedan or even many traditional pickup trucks. Parking garages, narrow streets, and tight parking spots can feel like a challenge. It's not the most practical choice for someone who needs to navigate congested city environments daily.

Inside, the Cybertruck offers a minimalist, utilitarian design. There's plenty of space, especially in the cabin, with seating for up to six people. The front seats are comfortable, and the layout is straightforward, with all controls housed in a single large touchscreen. The cabin is spacious, providing ample legroom for front and rear passengers. However, the interior might not have the same level of plush luxury found in some high-end vehicles, as Tesla opted for a more rugged, industrial look that matches the exterior. The seats are made of durable materials, designed to withstand wear and tear, which is great for practicality, but they might not have the level of comfort some people are used to in more premium vehicles.

Storage is another area where the Cybertruck shines. In addition to the large bed, there's a front trunk (or "frunk") that offers ample space for carrying smaller items. It's perfect for stowing groceries, bags, or anything you might want to keep out of sight. However, because of the Cybertruck's unique design, the frunk is a bit unconventional compared to other electric vehicles. It's not as deep as some might expect, but it's still a practical addition for people who need extra storage.

Ultimately, the Cybertruck's practicality comes down to how you intend to use it. If you need a vehicle that can handle rough terrain, tow heavy loads, or transport large items, the Cybertruck is a fantastic choice. It's more than capable of meeting those needs. But for daily use in urban settings, especially in tighter spaces, it might not be the most practical option. It's a truck that makes a bold statement, but it's not necessarily the easiest vehicle to integrate into a busy, city-centered lifestyle. For those who have the space and need for a rugged, electric truck, though, it's an incredibly capable and unique machine.

When it comes to technology, the Cybertruck is, as expected, packed with the cutting-edge features that have become synonymous with Tesla. The centerpiece of its tech suite is Tesla's famous Autopilot system, which offers semi-autonomous driving capabilities. While I don't trust it to handle everything—especially on more complex roads—I did get a chance to test it during long stretches of highway driving. The system, which uses a combination of cameras, sensors, and machine learning to steer, brake, and accelerate, performs surprisingly well. The Cybertruck kept a steady lane, adjusted speed based on traffic, and even took gentle turns when needed. It's not quite the fully self-driving experience Tesla envisions for the future, but it's an impressive step in that direction.

The interior of the Cybertruck is another area where Tesla shines, particularly with the user interface. The dashboard is dominated by a massive touchscreen display that controls almost every aspect of the vehicle, from climate control to navigation to even controlling the seats. It's a minimalist design that feels ultra-modern, with very few physical buttons to distract you. At first, the lack of tactile controls was a little disorienting, but after some time, I came to appreciate the simplicity of it all. The touchscreen is incredibly responsive, and Tesla's software updates continue to improve functionality, adding new features and fine-tuning existing ones. The system integrates seamlessly with your phone, so you can control a lot of the vehicle's features remotely—whether it's unlocking the doors or pre-conditioning the cabin for a comfortable ride.

Then there's the innovation in things like the onboard cameras, which provide a 360-degree view around the vehicle, and the ability to remotely monitor the charging process through the Tesla app. It's the kind of convenience and tech integration that makes the Cybertruck feel like more than just a car—it feels like a mobile extension of your life. Features like the advanced climate system, ambient lighting, and adjustable air suspension only add to the sense of luxury and forward-thinking that the Cybertruck brings to the table.

However, for all the promise of Tesla's tech, there have been a few bumps along the road. The most glaring issue I encountered was the charging problems. From the very first time I tried to charge the truck, I ran into unexpected errors. The connection didn't always work as smoothly as it should, and the truck's software occasionally displayed charging faults, which added unnecessary stress to what should have been a simple process. This was especially frustrating considering how integral Tesla's supercharger network is to the whole experience—if the charging issues hadn't been resolved, it would have severely impacted the usability of the vehicle.

Another issue I encountered was related to the build quality. While the Cybertruck's exterior is made from ultra-tough stainless steel, which is an impressive feat of engineering, I did notice some inconsistencies in the fit and finish of certain components. Some panels didn't line up perfectly, and there were small gaps or misalignments in places that would usually be hidden in more traditionally designed cars. These issues weren't deal-breakers, but they did make me question whether the Cybertruck was ready for the mass market in terms of quality control. It wasn't a matter of functionality—everything worked as it should—it was more about the attention to detail that was sometimes lacking.

Then there was the matter of customer support. While Tesla has a reputation for being quick with software updates and addressing technical problems remotely, getting timely help for more hands-on issues wasn't always straightforward. There were moments when I needed assistance with minor issues or troubleshooting, and while the Tesla support team was knowledgeable, it took longer than I would have liked to get a resolution. In a vehicle this groundbreaking, where users are essentially pioneers in terms of ownership, the need for a more responsive, efficient support system was more apparent than ever. Tesla has certainly made strides in improving its customer service, but there's still room for growth in terms of providing more personal, accessible assistance when issues arise.

Despite these setbacks, the overall experience of driving the Cybertruck remains incredibly exciting, and I believe that Tesla will continue to refine both the technology and the quality of the vehicle with time. For anyone considering purchasing a Cybertruck, it's important to be aware of these challenges—especially in the early stages of ownership—so that you're prepared to address them as they arise. However, the potential of the Cybertruck as a game-changing vehicle is undeniable, and as with any cutting-edge technology, there are bound to be a few growing pains along the way.

Chapter 6: The Bold Experiment of Tesla

Tesla's decision to bring the Cybertruck to market was nothing short of a bold gamble—one that challenged not just the automotive industry but the very perception of what a vehicle should be. Traditional truck designs have remained largely the same for decades, with incremental improvements in performance, comfort, and efficiency, but the overall form has stuck to familiar formulas. Pickup trucks are often defined by their ruggedness, utility, and a certain level of conservatism in design. They are built to appeal to a broad audience, and as such, their designs have often followed a predictable pattern. But with the Cybertruck, Tesla flipped that script entirely.

The Cybertruck's angular, stainless steel exoskeleton is a direct challenge to conventional truck aesthetics. Instead of curves, polished chrome, and sleek lines, the Cybertruck presents a geometric, almost industrial look that's both jarring and captivating. It looks more like a vehicle you'd see in a science fiction movie or a post-apocalyptic world than anything that's currently on the road. This design is a statement—a rejection of the norms that have defined the automotive industry for over a century. Where most automakers are focused on refining their existing models, Tesla pushed forward with something radically different, something that forced people to look at trucks—and vehicles in general—in a completely new way.

One of the most intriguing aspects of Tesla's gamble with the Cybertruck is how the design challenges our ideas of strength and durability. The truck's body is made from ultra-hard stainless steel, a material that's both incredibly tough and resistant to dents and scratches, something that sets it apart from traditional truck bodies made of aluminum or sheet metal. This material choice alone signals Tesla's intention to do things differently, aiming for a vehicle that's more about function than form—practicality over tradition. The decision to make the truck bulletproof, with windows designed to withstand impacts (despite the famous mishap during the reveal), is just another way Tesla has redefined what a truck can be. It's not just a workhorse; it's a fortress on wheels.

But Tesla's gamble isn't just about the truck's exterior. The Cybertruck represents a challenge to the traditional automotive business model as well. From the outset, it was clear that Tesla wasn't going to take the usual path of building a car and then relying on dealerships and conventional marketing to sell it. The direct-to-consumer sales model, combined with online preorders, bypasses much of the traditional distribution channels that other automakers still rely on. The result is a more streamlined approach to getting the product into customers' hands—one that is more in line with Tesla's philosophy of innovation and disruption.

Tesla's gamble with the Cybertruck is also a reflection of the company's broader vision for the future of transportation. Elon Musk has long been vocal about his goal to push humanity toward sustainable energy, and the Cybertruck is part of that grand vision. The vehicle isn't just electric for the sake of being electric; it's a part of Musk's larger mission to create a sustainable, eco-friendly transportation ecosystem. The Cybertruck's durability, combined with Tesla's electric powertrain, makes it a potential game-changer in industries like construction, farming, and outdoor adventure. It's a vehicle that challenges the idea that electric cars are only for urban environments or those looking for a low-impact commute. The Cybertruck, with its impressive towing capacity, off-road capabilities, and rugged design, is an electric vehicle built for hard work, for people who need power and versatility—without the fossil fuels.

In essence, Tesla's vision with the Cybertruck isn't just about creating a vehicle that breaks from tradition; it's about reshaping the entire paradigm of what a car can and should be. It's a gamble that, for better or worse, is forcing the automotive world to rethink what is possible, and it's doing so with the same blend of audacity and ambition that has defined Tesla from the start. The Cybertruck is far more than just another electric vehicle—it's a vehicle built for the future, a future that's bound to look very different from the present. Whether it succeeds or falters, it's clear that the Cybertruck is a sign of things to come, and that Tesla is unapologetically leading the charge.

The Cybertruck represents more than just a new vehicle from Tesla; it is a key player in the ongoing disruption of the automotive industry. For decades, the car industry has been slow to change, dominated by legacy brands and entrenched manufacturing processes. But Tesla, under the visionary leadership of Elon Musk, has not only challenged this status quo but actively sought to dismantle it. The Cybertruck, with its unconventional design and ambitious promises, is a prime example of how Tesla is shifting the narrative surrounding electric vehicles (EVs) and the broader automotive market.

For years, the mainstream narrative around EVs focused on their eco-friendly benefits and the desire to reduce our reliance on fossil fuels. However, this conversation was largely dominated by smaller, more "traditional" vehicles—sedans, hatchbacks, and crossovers—that prioritized efficiency over emotional appeal. The Cybertruck, on the other hand, has taken a completely different approach. It doesn't just offer an electric alternative to gasoline-powered trucks; it redefines the very idea of what a truck should be, merging cutting-edge electric technology with radical design choices. This is about more than just sustainability; it's about creating an entirely new kind of vehicle, one that speaks to the future, one that challenges consumers to think about transportation in a radically different way.

Tesla's influence on the EV space is undeniable, and the Cybertruck is just the beginning. With the popularity of the Cybertruck growing, it's clear that traditional automakers are beginning to take notice.

Companies like Ford and Rivian have already released electric trucks to compete, but none have captured the same level of attention or enthusiasm as Tesla's creation. In many ways, the Cybertruck has set the bar—not just for electric trucks but for what consumers can expect from the future of automobiles. Tesla is proving that EVs can be more than just a niche market—they can appeal to those who have long been loyal to gas-powered vehicles, including those in industries like construction, agriculture, and transportation that rely on the power and utility of pickup trucks.

Looking toward the future, it's exciting to speculate how Tesla will continue to push the boundaries with future models of the Cybertruck. There's no doubt that Tesla will refine and improve upon the existing design, especially addressing some of the challenges that have arisen with the first iteration. One area where future models may see significant improvements is in the charging infrastructure. The early issues I encountered with charging are likely to be addressed in later versions, both in terms of charging speed and compatibility with a wider range of stations. Tesla's aggressive push to expand its Supercharger network will likely play a key role in making the Cybertruck—and EVs in general—more accessible and practical for daily use.

In addition, while the Cybertruck's performance is already exceptional, further enhancements in terms of range and efficiency can be expected. As battery technology improves, Tesla will likely be able to offer even longer ranges and faster charging times, making the Cybertruck a more viable option for long road trips and heavy-duty usage. As autonomous driving technology matures, we may also see future Cybertrucks equipped with more advanced versions of Tesla's Autopilot system, moving closer to full self-driving capability. Features like remote driving, improved safety systems, and smarter onboard AI could become standard, further pushing the boundaries of what's possible with a vehicle.

The Cybertruck, in many ways, represents a living blueprint—a constantly evolving product that will continue to shape the future of transportation. Whether it's refining the exterior design, improving interior comforts, or enhancing technological capabilities, the next iterations will likely address many of the teething problems that have emerged with the first version. For Tesla, the challenge is not just about building the best truck; it's about continuing to lead the charge in a rapidly changing automotive landscape. And with the Cybertruck already disrupting the industry, it's clear that the company is just getting started. The future of cars is electric, and the Cybertruck is paving the way for a new era of bold, innovative, and sustainable transportation.

Chapter 7: The Ownership Experience

Owning the Cybertruck every day has been nothing short of a unique experience. From the moment I took possession of it, I knew that this was no ordinary vehicle—it was going to impact my day-to-day life in ways I hadn't fully anticipated. It's one thing to drive a futuristic car for a test spin or a weekend getaway, but it's another thing entirely to make it a part of your daily routine. As the first Cybertruck owner in the UK, I quickly discovered that this truck wasn't just a game-changer for Tesla or the automotive industry—it was a game-changer for my lifestyle.

The first thing that became apparent was the size. The Cybertruck is massive. At over 5 meters long and more than 2 meters wide, it dominates the roads. Navigating tight spaces, especially in urban areas or places where parking is limited, became an immediate challenge. The truck is wider than most standard parking spaces, so I found myself constantly looking for larger spaces, often in more remote areas or spots that weren't the most convenient. I quickly learned to adjust my expectations when it came to parking. It wasn't uncommon for me to walk a few extra blocks just to park the truck without worrying about door dings or tight squeezes.

But the size also has its advantages. The bed of the truck is huge—big enough to accommodate large pieces of furniture, bikes, or other bulky items that I would have struggled to fit in any other vehicle. I've made several trips to the hardware store, loaded it up with tools and supplies, and realized just how much more useful a pickup can be when it's electric. There's no gas to worry about, no engine noise, and the trunk space is vast, providing room for everything from camping gear to large DIY projects. The sheer utility of the Cybertruck is one of its standout features. The bed is lined with durable material and designed to withstand heavy loads, and the tailgate's smart design allows for easy access. This makes hauling things not just easier, but more enjoyable—especially when you factor in the instantaneous torque that comes with an electric vehicle. When I'm loading heavy items, I don't have to deal with the traditional grunting that comes with a gas-powered engine struggling under a load. The Cybertruck just...does it.

However, there are trade-offs. While the Cybertruck is incredibly efficient when it comes to power and performance, the reality of charging remains a practical issue that every EV owner must deal with. Living with the Cybertruck means planning your charging sessions carefully, especially during longer trips. If you're used to the convenience of a gas station every few miles, it takes some getting used to the fact that charging stations for electric vehicles are still fewer and farther between, particularly outside of major cities. Planning a road trip in the Cybertruck involves mapping out supercharger stations along the route and factoring in the time it takes to juice up the battery. The process has become more streamlined over time, but it's still not as instantaneous as refueling with gas.

The interior is another aspect that impacts daily life. Tesla's minimalist design philosophy means that there are very few distractions inside the truck—no buttons, no knobs, just a massive touchscreen that controls everything. This can be a bit disorienting at first, especially if you're used to a more traditional dashboard. However, over time, I came to appreciate the simplicity and ease of use. Everything is intuitive, and the integration with the Tesla app makes controlling the vehicle from a distance incredibly convenient. Whether it's checking the charge level, pre-conditioning the cabin on a cold morning, or even using the app to unlock the truck remotely, Tesla's technology makes ownership feel seamless.

Comfort is another area where the Cybertruck exceeds expectations. Despite its rugged, industrial exterior, the ride is smooth, quiet, and surprisingly plush. Tesla's air suspension system does an excellent job of smoothing out bumpy roads, and while the interior is utilitarian, it's also spacious and surprisingly comfortable. The seating is supportive for long drives, and the cabin, while sparse in its design, feels futuristic in its openness. The large windows and high driving position provide great visibility, which makes driving a truck of this size feel less intimidating than you might expect.

Living with the Cybertruck means experiencing a vehicle that constantly reminds you that you're part of a technological leap forward. It's not just a vehicle—it's an experience, one that makes everyday tasks like running errands, going to the grocery store, or even just taking the kids to school feel like something out of the ordinary. The Cybertruck's presence on the road is unavoidable, and it sparks conversations wherever it goes. Whether it's a question about its electric powertrain, the unique design, or just the overall driving experience, the Cybertruck always brings a sense of excitement and curiosity to the mundane moments of life.

But that's what makes it special. The Cybertruck isn't just a car; it's a daily reminder that we are witnessing the future of transportation unfold before our eyes. While it's not without its quirks—issues with charging, its massive size, and the ongoing challenge of fitting it into the infrastructure—it's clear that living with the Cybertruck is never boring. It's a constant adventure, and for those who want to be part of something bigger than themselves, it offers an ownership experience like no other.

Dealing with Issues

Owning the first Cybertruck in the UK has not come without its challenges, particularly when it comes to dealing with some of the vehicle's teething problems. While the truck's design and performance are impressive, it's the issues—many of them typical of a first-generation vehicle—that tend to draw the most attention.

One of the most significant hurdles I faced early on was with charging. While the Cybertruck is designed to work seamlessly with Tesla's network of Superchargers, I quickly discovered that finding a charging station in certain areas was not always straightforward. The UK, despite its growing EV infrastructure, still doesn't have the same density of charging points as other parts of Europe. As the Cybertruck is larger than most vehicles, the extra space required to park near a charger only adds to the complexity. It's not always easy to find a charger that can accommodate such a large vehicle without taking up multiple spaces.

Even when I did manage to find a suitable charger, there were times when the charging process didn't go as smoothly as expected. From connectivity errors to charging stations being out of order, I found that some of the convenience I had come to expect from Tesla's ecosystem wasn't always guaranteed. The charging infrastructure, while extensive, still feels like a work in progress in certain regions, and the early adoption of the Cybertruck sometimes felt like an experiment in itself, with various bumps along the way.

Another issue I encountered was related to the truck's connectivity. While the Tesla app allows you to remotely monitor and control many of the vehicle's functions, there were moments when the app would fail to sync properly with the truck, or updates would take longer than expected. It's a small annoyance, but in a world where immediate access to technology is expected, it was a reminder that the Cybertruck is, in many ways, still finding its feet in terms of software integration.

And then there was the infamous "charging error" I experienced early on. I spent hours troubleshooting, trying different chargers, and seeking assistance from Tesla support. Although the customer service team was helpful, the process felt far more cumbersome than I anticipated for a vehicle as advanced as the Cybertruck. It was a reminder that, despite its cutting-edge technology, the car still had room for improvement.

Financial Aspects

Owning a Cybertruck is an exciting, yet costly, venture—one that requires careful financial consideration. While the upfront cost of the vehicle is high, it's the hidden costs that can catch new owners off guard. The base model of the Cybertruck, even with its impressive features, comes with a price tag that can reach upwards of £40,000, and that's before factoring in additional upgrades like enhanced autopilot or higher performance models. For many, this is a significant investment, and it's worth carefully weighing whether the vehicle's unique advantages justify the steep price.

Beyond the initial purchase, the costs don't stop there. One of the major savings the Cybertruck offers is in fuel. As an electric vehicle, it eliminates the need for gasoline or diesel, which can make it significantly cheaper to run over time compared to a traditional internal combustion engine truck. Charging at home, especially during off-peak hours, can bring down costs even further. However, this savings is somewhat offset by the potential costs of maintaining the vehicle's specialized systems. While Tesla vehicles are generally known for their low maintenance requirements, the sheer scale of the Cybertruck means that any repairs or parts replacements—especially for specialized components like its stainless-steel body—could be pricier than you might expect for a traditional truck.

Another potential hidden cost comes in the form of insurance. Given the Cybertruck's large size, premium technology, and novelty status, insurance premiums tend to be higher than average. While the vehicle is built to be durable, accidents or collisions with such a unique vehicle could be more costly to repair than a typical truck. Additionally, some insurers may charge higher rates for electric vehicles, even though the Cybertruck is more durable than many traditional trucks in terms of bodywork.

There are also the costs associated with the vehicle's unique size. The Cybertruck's large proportions mean that some places—especially older or more cramped urban areas—might require additional expenses for parking or public access. In some cases, you may find that your parking spaces are limited or more expensive due to the vehicle's footprint. This is an added financial consideration, especially if you live in a city with tight parking regulations.

Lastly, while Tesla's Supercharger network is extensive, it's important to note that relying solely on these charging stations outside of home charging can add up, especially on longer road trips. Although Superchargers offer fast charging, the cost per charge can vary depending on location, and frequent use may add unexpected costs over time.

As I found out, the costs of charging can fluctuate depending on the region, with some areas charging higher rates than others.

In the grand scheme of things, owning the Cybertruck represents a long-term investment. Its electric nature ensures lower ongoing running costs compared to a gas-powered truck, but there are still substantial initial and potential maintenance costs to consider. If you're prepared for the upfront expense and ongoing ownership costs, the Cybertruck can offer a truly unique experience—but it's important to be fully aware of these financial factors before making the leap.

Chapter 8: Possible Solutions and What Tesla Needs to Improve

When it comes to the Cybertruck, charging issues were one of the most immediate challenges I faced. Despite being part of the Tesla family, the sheer size and demand for charging infrastructure made some early experiences more frustrating than anticipated. However, there were workarounds and solutions that helped alleviate these challenges.

For starters, one of the most obvious solutions was simply planning ahead. Tesla's Supercharger network is extensive, but it's not as ubiquitous as gas stations. In rural or less populated areas, finding a nearby station can be tricky. Using the in-car navigation to locate Superchargers and checking them for availability through the Tesla app became a regular part of the journey. Another handy feature Tesla offers is the ability to reserve a charging spot. It's a useful tool when traveling long distances, ensuring that a charging station is available upon arrival.

When the Supercharger network wasn't an option or I was dealing with an issue at a specific station, third-party charging solutions came into play. Tesla offers an adapter for non-Tesla charging stations, allowing the Cybertruck to charge at many of the UK's other EV chargers. These are often found at locations like motorway service areas, shopping malls, and public car parks. However, not all of these third-party chargers offer the same charging speed as Tesla's own network, and some may not be as reliable. Compatibility is still improving, and the experience isn't always as seamless, but it provides a viable backup when needed.

There are also several home charging solutions, which, for someone who drives the Cybertruck daily, became essential. Installing a Level 2 charger at home was a no-brainer for me. The convenience of waking up to a fully charged truck every day, without having to rely solely on public stations, was a game-changer. The installation process was straightforward enough, but it does come at an upfront cost, as it requires a special power outlet to handle the truck's charging needs.

Despite these solutions, charging the Cybertruck does require a bit more planning and thought than a traditional vehicle. It's not something you can take for granted, especially when driving long distances or in areas with limited infrastructure. But with a bit of preparation and the right tools, the charging issues are manageable.

As much as I love the design of the Cybertruck, no vehicle is without its flaws. There were a few design quirks that became apparent over time—some of which are functional limitations that could be improved upon in future models. For example, while the truck's exterior is undeniably striking, the stainless steel body can be prone to scratches and dings. Despite being incredibly durable, it lacks the "forgiving" nature of softer materials like aluminum. Every small scratch felt like a reminder of just how unique the material is. The absence of paint is also a double-edged sword: While it means the body is more resistant to rust and corrosion, it also makes any imperfections stand out more than they might on traditional vehicles. Tesla is offering some solutions to this with paint protection films and other coatings, but these are additional costs that owners need to consider.

Another aspect I found challenging was the lack of some traditional features that are often expected in trucks. The Cybertruck's angular design, while futuristic and eye-catching, can make loading and unloading cargo a bit tricky. The bed itself is enormous, but the absence of a traditional tailgate that can easily lower to allow for a smooth, wide-open space for loading was a bit limiting. While the truck's bed is durable and spacious, a more user-friendly design could improve the practicality of transporting larger items, especially when you need to load or unload by yourself.

The interior, while sleek and minimalistic, lacks some of the functional touches that make everyday use of a vehicle easier. For example, the glove compartment is smaller than you'd expect, and there's limited storage space inside the cabin for everyday items like water bottles or snacks. Given the truck's size and purpose, these small annoyances are easy to overlook, but they highlight the trade-off between futuristic design and practical, everyday use.

There's also the matter of the Cybertruck's visibility. While the angular exterior is a hallmark of its design, the large rear pillars can create blind spots, particularly when reversing or changing lanes. Tesla's advanced camera system helps alleviate some of these issues, but in terms of traditional vehicle design, the visibility could be improved for enhanced safety and ease of driving.

All in all, the Cybertruck is a vehicle that redefines what a truck can be, but like any early iteration of a groundbreaking product, it's not perfect. As Tesla continues to refine the vehicle, these design concerns will likely be addressed in future models, offering owners an even more polished version of what is already a game-changing vehicle.

When it comes to customer support, Tesla's reputation is a bit of a mixed bag. On the one hand, their customer service team is generally responsive, especially when it comes to handling technical issues or providing guidance on features. When I encountered some of the initial charging difficulties, reaching out to Tesla's support team was surprisingly easy. They were quick to help troubleshoot the issue, walking me through potential fixes and providing updates on station availability. Their approach is often more digital-first, with many support requests handled via the app or online, which can feel efficient for straightforward problems.

However, the real test came when I needed physical support—like scheduling a repair or getting hands-on assistance with issues that couldn't be solved remotely. In these instances, the experience became less seamless. For a vehicle like the

Cybertruck, which is still in its early stages of ownership, getting a timely appointment for repairs or even for routine maintenance can sometimes feel like a wait-and-see game. The challenge of Tesla's expanding customer base combined with the newness of the Cybertruck model means that some service centers can become overwhelmed, leaving owners like me waiting longer than anticipated for repairs or updates.

Another challenge I faced was the communication between different Tesla departments. For instance, while one team might quickly resolve a software issue over the phone or via app support, I'd sometimes need to follow up with another department regarding parts or delivery. The lack of a seamless handoff between teams was frustrating at times, especially when it came to resolving more complicated issues.

While the experience is generally positive and offers a level of support that's better than many traditional automakers, there are certainly areas that could use improvement. One suggestion would be expanding Tesla's service infrastructure to ensure quicker and more widespread access to repairs and physical support, particularly for early adopters like myself. Making sure that every service center has a well-trained team capable of handling Cybertruck-specific issues could help mitigate delays and improve the overall ownership experience.

As for enhancing the overall experience, there are a few areas where Tesla could do even more. For example, I think the app could be further refined to offer more granular control over vehicle settings and diagnostics. While the current version allows you to monitor charging and access certain functions, a more detailed diagnostic feature—showing real-time health reports on everything from battery life to mechanical components—would help owners stay ahead of potential problems. Additionally, expanding Tesla's remote service options could reduce the need for in-person visits, speeding up the process of getting issues resolved. A more proactive approach, where Tesla provides automatic updates about the truck's performance or possible maintenance needs, would also be a welcome improvement.

Lastly, integrating more community-driven support options, such as a forum for owners to share insights, tips, and solutions to common problems, could help improve the overall experience. Tesla's community of fans and owners is vast, and tapping into that knowledge could lead to faster, more diverse solutions, especially for issues that don't require official support intervention. As the Cybertruck continues to evolve, I'm hopeful that Tesla will build on this early ownership experience, improving not only the vehicle itself but the infrastructure that supports it. After all, owning a game-changing truck like the Cybertruck is one thing, but ensuring that every moment of ownership is just as innovative is what will truly set it apart in the long run.

Chapter 9: Looking Ahead

As I reflect on my journey with the Cybertruck—both the highs and the inevitable hurdles—I find myself asking the same question many car enthusiasts, industry analysts, and potential buyers have: *Is the Cybertruck truly a game-changer?*

From the moment it was unveiled, the Cybertruck was met with skepticism, excitement, and intrigue. Its radical design was unlike anything seen in the automotive world, with its geometric, almost futuristic look throwing a wrench into the long-standing traditions of truck design. Tesla didn't just build a pickup; they built a statement—a vehicle that dared to redefine what a truck could be in the 21st century. It was a gamble that some might argue could either disrupt the market or flop dramatically. But after having spent significant time behind the wheel of this vehicle, I am inclined to say that the Cybertruck is indeed a game-changer.

The way the Cybertruck challenges traditional automotive design is revolutionary. It rejects the conventions of sleek curves and shiny chrome, opting instead for a bold, utilitarian, and, at times, almost alien aesthetic. But beyond the look, it is what's inside that truly sets it apart. The integration of cutting-edge electric technology, from its all-electric powertrain to its self-driving capabilities, is light-years ahead of what most traditional trucks offer. Tesla's commitment to sustainability through this vehicle—coupled with its innovation in performance, safety, and technology—marks a turning point not just for pickup trucks, but for the entire automotive industry.

The performance of the Cybertruck is equally disruptive. Tesla has managed to pack the power, speed, and handling of a sports car into a truck that is rugged enough to take on rough terrains and demanding tasks. In doing so, they have proven that EVs can not only compete with gas-powered vehicles but often outperform them. The Cybertruck is designed to be more than just a vehicle; it is a lifestyle, an adventure machine, and an eco-friendly powerhouse all in one. For those seeking a vehicle that can handle the toughest jobs while offering the benefits of clean energy, this is the ultimate solution.

But it's not just about performance and technology. The Cybertruck also addresses a market gap—one that blends traditional workhorse functionality with modern, futuristic features. The immense storage capacity, the durability of its stainless steel exoskeleton, and its innovative electric features cater to people who need a robust vehicle without sacrificing the cutting-edge tech that Tesla is known for. In short, it's a perfect blend of work and play, practicality and luxury.

However, no vehicle is without its flaws. The size of the Cybertruck, while appealing to those looking for a powerful, rugged truck, can also be a hindrance, especially in urban environments. Its charging challenges, despite Tesla's best efforts, remind us that the infrastructure to support such a massive and revolutionary vehicle is still in the process of catching up. The customer support experience, while generally good, could also be smoother, especially for early adopters who might encounter unique issues with a first-generation model.

Still, despite these hurdles, the Cybertruck is undeniably a game-changer. It pushes the boundaries of what's possible in the automotive world and sets the stage for what's to come in the era of electric vehicles. As more people get behind the wheel of the Cybertruck and experience its innovative design, performance, and practicality, it will undoubtedly continue to change perceptions of what a truck can be.

In the grander scheme, the Cybertruck is just one example of Tesla's ongoing disruption of the entire automotive industry. It serves as a powerful reminder that innovation doesn't come from following the rules—it comes from breaking them.

The Cybertruck's impact on the market, the industry, and even the culture at large cannot be understated. Whether you love it or hate it, there's no denying that it has shaken up the world of cars forever. And in the end, isn't that what a true game-changer does?

The arrival of the Cybertruck has already started to make waves, not only within the automotive industry but also within the larger movement toward sustainable transportation. Tesla has long been a pioneer in the electric vehicle (EV) space, and the Cybertruck represents a bold step forward in that mission. Its impact on the culture of EV ownership is undeniable, pushing the boundaries of what an electric vehicle can be, and challenging consumers to rethink their preconceived notions about trucks, electric power, and the future of transportation.

The Cybertruck's sheer presence is already shifting the conversation about EVs. For years, electric vehicles have been associated with compact sedans, hatchbacks, and luxury cars. There's an image of electric vehicles being efficient, eco-friendly alternatives for urban dwellers or those looking to reduce their carbon footprint. The Cybertruck, however, is reimagining the entire category. It's a big, bold, and undeniably cool vehicle that appeals not just to environmentalists but to truck enthusiasts, off-roaders, and even those who might have never considered going electric. By making electric power synonymous with strength and utility, the Cybertruck is opening the doors for a new class of EV owners. It's showing people that going green doesn't have to mean sacrificing power, performance, or ruggedness.

Tesla's gamble on the Cybertruck has the potential to drive mass adoption of electric vehicles in an entirely new demographic—people who value power and performance but are looking for an eco-conscious alternative. It's the kind of vehicle that could inspire the creation of similar models from other manufacturers, each attempting to match Tesla's bold approach to the future of transportation. As more automakers begin to see the popularity and potential of electric pickups, it's likely we'll see a wider variety of EVs designed for different niches, from off-road adventures to everyday urban driving.

As for advice for future owners of the Cybertruck, there are a few key things to keep in mind. First and foremost, understand that owning the first-generation model comes with its own set of challenges. It's an early adopter's vehicle, and as such, you should expect some growing pains. The technology is advanced, and while Tesla offers a fantastic network of updates and improvements through software patches, some of the hardware and functionality may still need time to be fine-tuned. Issues like charging compatibility, service access, and occasional glitches in connectivity may crop up, so it's crucial to be patient and proactive about resolving them.

Secondly, get familiar with the vehicle's charging needs early on. While Tesla's Supercharger network is one of the best in the world, it's not everywhere yet, particularly in some rural or less developed areas. Installing a home charging station is a must if you're planning to use the Cybertruck as your daily driver. This will ensure that you never have to worry about long charging times or finding an available charger when you're in a hurry.

Finally, embrace the uniqueness of the vehicle. The Cybertruck's design isn't for everyone, but it is undeniably a conversation starter. Everywhere you go, you'll attract attention—whether it's admiration, confusion, or even criticism. But that's the beauty of the Cybertruck. It doesn't blend in. It challenges perceptions, and as a result, it becomes part of the cultural conversation around electric vehicles and the future of sustainable transportation.

For those considering making the leap into Cybertruck ownership, the key is to be ready for an experience that's unlike anything else on the road.

It's not just about driving a truck—it's about embracing a new vision for the future. And while it may not be perfect right out of the gate, there's no denying that the Cybertruck is a glimpse into the future of what cars can—and should—be. If you're up for the ride, it's one worth taking.

Conclusion

Owning the first Cybertruck in the UK has been an experience that's difficult to summarize in just a few words. It's been a journey of highs and lows, moments of sheer excitement balanced with moments of frustration. But above all, it's been a reminder of why we take risks in the first place—because sometimes, the rewards are worth it. I didn't just buy a truck; I bought a piece of automotive history, a vehicle that's as much about shaping the future as it is about getting from point A to point B.

Reflecting on the journey, I can honestly say that the Cybertruck has lived up to its promise in many ways. Its bold design, unparalleled performance, and Tesla's innovative technology have made it a game-changer in every sense of the word. Of course, there were challenges along the way—charging issues, minor glitches, and the occasional public skepticism—but those are the realities of being an early adopter. I knew what I was getting into, and despite the obstacles, I wouldn't change the experience for anything.

For anyone considering whether the Cybertruck is the right fit for them, it really depends on what you're looking for in a vehicle. If you're someone who needs a rugged, powerful vehicle that can handle heavy-duty tasks while also making a statement, then the Cybertruck might be exactly what you need. Its performance, design, and utility are second to none in the EV space. On the other hand, if you're primarily looking for something compact, easy to park, and low-maintenance, you might want to think twice. The Cybertruck's sheer size can be a challenge, especially in urban environments where parking is tight. And while the Cybertruck is a stunning vehicle, it's not necessarily for those who want something that blends into the background.

Ultimately, the Cybertruck isn't just a vehicle; it's a movement. It represents a bold vision of the future, one where electric vehicles are not only the sustainable choice but also the thrilling, practical, and desirable option. As for the road ahead, Tesla's journey is far from over. The success of the Cybertruck could pave the way for an entire generation of electric trucks, SUVs, and even commercial vehicles. It's a glimpse into the future of transportation, where the possibilities are endless. And as someone who's fortunate enough to be along for the ride, I can say with confidence: the future looks electric.

www.ingramcontent.com/pod-product-compliance
Lightning Source LLC
Chambersburg PA
CBHW071106240526
45469CB00006BD/2343